LEARNING TEST AND PSYCHOLOGY

INTERVIEW SKILLS

JOHN LOK

Copyright

Contents

Preface

I write this book aims to let interviewers to know why to apply pshological methods to judge how to choose the most suitable applicant(s) more accurate to any organization in any interviews. This book consists two parts. The first part concerns to explain what the different interview methods can be used to evaluate whom is the mos right applicant.

In the first part, it explains what the different common interview methods are. The first chapter indicates what the common interviews are as well as explains why interviewers need to apply psychological methods to test any applicant behaviors in any interview process. The second chapter explains how to apply psychological recruitment strategies effect/manage in the recruitment process to achieve more effective and efficient interview as well as explains how to apply occupational psychological test method to test applicant's ability. The third chapter how selection assessment methods are applied to choose the best applicants to achieve the most effective and efficient interview result as well as how to criteria for selecting and evaluating assessment methods in interview which are the most reasonable support. The four charper explains how to apply suitational questions to select the most right applicant to do management position.

The second part explains what the psychological interviews are , it concerns challenge of HR management it is as a HR specialist, what are the challenges you may face and what HR intervention mechanisms would you consider using in an attempt to drive individual and organization performance in a multinational company? Critically evaluate this question by utilizing the appropriate academic literatures.

The challenges of the HR specialist when there engage in attempt of increasing the individual and organization performances in Multinational companies through developing a set of HRM best practices, especially relating to employee recruitment and selection, performance management and staff retention. Since the organizations are multinational number of concerns are arises such as dealing cultural issues with the organizational goals as well as individual goals.

Prologue

Table Of Contents

Test interview methods

ONE

INTERVIEW PSYCHOLOGY METHODS

What are common psychology methods of recruitment choice? Can any psychology methods are used to choose who will be the best recruitment applicant(s) in any recruitment stage more accurate? Can the interviewer observe the applicant's psychological phenomenon to judge whether the applicant can be the best or the most suitable applicant in the recruitment stage more accurate? To answer above these questions. We need to know why a systematic scientific procedure is an essential component to achieve any psychological method(s) to test candidate individual ability to judge whether who is the best or the most suitable applicant to do any position in any organization.

A psychologist can follow a systematic scientific procedure which has theoretical base in order to explain and interpret the psychological phenomenon of the applicant to decide whether who is the best or the most suitable applicant to do the position in the organization.

On the one hand, in order to obtain the applicant's psychological response from individual applicant, there are a number of psychological tools or instruments are used during the interview process. The responses are taken on these tools constitute the basic data which are analyzed to study the applicant experiences, e.g. working experiences, life experiences, mental processes and behaviors. On the other hand, in order to understand every applicant's behavior during the interview process. The different psychological methods can be applied for solving different applicant's individual behavior (individual mental problems) to judge who will be the best or the most suitable applicant to the position in any organization. Because different situations will cause the applicant to choose how to do or perform different behaviors to persuade the interviewer believes who is the best or the most suitable applicant to do the position in the organization. Thus, whose performances will be shaped by many factors both intrinsic and extrinsic to him or her in any interview process.

The common psychological methods of interview process include such as: For observation psychological method example, when shopping in the market , the researcher must have noticed various activities of the consumers . When he/she observes the consumers their activities, the researcher also think about as to why who are doing those activities and probably the researcher reaches a conclusion about the causes of such activities. So, observation is as a psychological method of enquiry is often understand as a systematic registering of events without any deliberate attempt to interface with variables operating in the event which is being studies.

Thus, observation psychological method seems to be applied to judge who is the best or the most suitable applicant to do any position in any organization in any interview process. Such as in any interview process, the interviewer (observer) can use this method to judge or observe every applicant's face and behavioral performance to feel whether who is the best or the most suitable applicant who own ability or confidence or qualification or experience to already to do the job to achieve the recruitment result is more accurate. For example, the interviewer (observer) can attempt to give one simple or difficult task to test whether whom the applicant has the more effort of the induced stress on task performance in the short time observation test in the on part stage of the interview process.

However, observation is also divided into either participant or non-participant both types, depending on the role of observer (interviewer). In the case of interview participant observation, the interviewer mixes up with the job (task) performance event test under study and conducts concerns the interview test, e.g. group discussion interview test, the applicants and the interviewer will discuss one or more than one topic(s) which concern(s) on relating the position requirement issue. So, the interviewer can analyze whom applicant(s) can talk the most reasonable evidences to support whose opinions to argue the topic against the other applicants together among of them in the short time group discussion, e.g. between 15 minutes to 30 minutes. It aims to let the interviewer can have enough time to record whose opinions to analyze whose opinions are the most reasonable argument to support whose main points to win this position among these interview competitors in the short time group discussion. Thus, the interviewer needs to participate the group discussion to ask every applicant any questions and let them to attempt to solve any challenges in the whole group discussion. After the group discussion, then the interviewer can have more effort or confidence to judge whom applicant (s) is/are the most suitable or the best applicant (s) to do the job for his/her organization more accurate.

Otherwise, as in the case of interview non-participant observation, the interviewer maintains an optimum distance and has little impact on the interview event. Such as the interview group discussion test. The interviewer won't ask any questions to let the applicants to attempt to answer. Otherwise, he/she will let the applicants have chance to ask any questions or answer the questions among of their discussion related to the topic. So the interviewer's role is a listener, who only needs to listen every applicant how who can ask and can answer any questions to decide who can talk the most correct or the right or the most reasonable answers to answer their questions in the short time group discussion. Then, the interviewer can record all applicants' questions and answers to make the judgement to decide who will be the right or the most suitable applicant to do the position in her/him organization more accurate.

● Why does need to test the applicant's psychological behavior in the interview process?

To answer this question, we need to know why any large or middle size organizations which need have human resource department. To challenge of today's HR managers is to create a pool of good employees in the organization. It starts from selection process of the employees. So, interview has been used as an important selection method by HR managers for long time. The cost of rehiring the importance of hiring the right person for right position first. It requires a reliable and valid interview process. Although, any interview won't guarantee 100 percent success in hiring the best employees into any organization, but the proper application is at least, will improve the chances of hiring the best applicant for the job the organization. The importance is given to the selection of right employees for the right positions. Firms are now realizing the value of the good employees because who can make a difference through their job performance. So, various selection methods are now being used to identify the right candidate.

" Interview" has emerged as a very useful tool in this regard. It is a very common selection method and has a high predictive validity for job performance (Robertson, & Smith , 2001). The main purpose of the interview is to select the right candidate for the right job. The importance of conducting an effective interview is also rising. So consensus was found among the HR experts regarding the effective interview techniques. There are a number of existing literatures regarding the techniques of an effective interview, but every few literatures exist regarding a systematic approach of conducting exist regarding a systematic approach of conducting an effective interview. This is a very few literatures exist regarding a complete interview process that shows a clear path to the employers for selecting right employees. A lot of interview technique are available, but the problem arises regarding the use of these techniques in a concrete manner. A systematic approach of interview will facilitate the tasks of HR managers in selecting the right applicant for the right position.

(Stevens, 1997) author indicated the whole process of the interview has been described in terms of "3D"-Development, discussion and decision. This study is particularly important for three reasons. First , it will help the HR mangers to think about the employee selection interview in a concrete manner. Second, it will help them to use a number of interview techniques in an effective way that will ultimately increase the chance of hiring the right person for the right position. Third, it will enrich the existing literature of selection interview.

(Stevens, 1997) author also explained that the growing importance of good employees will cause a challenge to the HR managers. The selection process of today's HR manager is becoming complex and challenging. Undoubtedly, the overall aim, of the selection process is to identify the candidates who are suitable for the vacancy or wider requirement of the HR plan. " Interview" has been used as a ' critical selection method ' by HR managers. The interview is the most valid method in determining an applicant's organizational fit, level of motivation and inter-personal selects.

Whetton & Cameron (2002) cited steps of process of conducting an interview, what they named as People-oriented selection interview process. Here is explains the interview process: P=prepare, E=establish rapport, O=obtain information, P=provide information, C= lead top close and E= evaluate.

So, it seems that the candidates' behavior individual performance in the interview process can be predicted whether who is(are) the most suitable or the best to do the position in the organization from the interviewer's observation. So, it also means the candidate's attitude in the interview process can perform to let the interviewer to feel whether who is suitable or the best to do the position in the organization . Thus, observation of the applicant individual performance, it is an interviewer's best interest to find good prospects, hire them and have them stay in the organization.

Therefore, the interviewees are needed to be provided sufficient information about the job and organization to have enough time to prepare before who will go to interview fairly. It aims to let every candidate has enough confidence to prepare to answer any questions in further interview process fairly. So, the development stage is a good preparation for the interview facilitates the effective interview process. To aim to let the candidate have enough preparation to interview , it should begin long before the first question is ever asked fairly.

In conclude, HR department seems an essential department to any middle or large organizations nowadays. It does not attribute only recruitment function to any organization, it also attribute the chance to give one psychological test function to evaluate whom applicant has the more experience and qualification and effort to do any position in any organization. If the interviewer has not prepared any psychological method to test any applicants to judge whether who has the more effort to do the position. Then, I believe the interview result will be more failure and more inaccurate to employ the most suitable applicant , due to who lacks the enough effort and qualification and experience to perform to finish any tasks or duties of the position . So, it is important why any organization needs have good psychological method to test and observe the applicant's psychological behavior in the interview process?

TWO

OCCUPATION PSYCHOLOGICAL TEST METHODS

How to apply psychological recruitment strategies effect/ manage in the recruitment process? HR (human resource) managers understand accept that poor recruitment decisions continue to affect organizational performance and limit goal achievement. In this case, many jurisdictions to identify and implement new effective hiring strategies will be serious issue to any HR departments to concern.

Acquiring and retaining high-quality talent is critical to any organization's success. So, recruiters need to be more elective in their choice. Since poor recruiting decisions can produce long term negative effects, among their high training and development costs to minimise the incidence of poor performance and high turnover to impact staff morale, the production of high quality goods and services. Thus, HR managers must seek all possible methods for improve their output and provide the satisfaction to their clients require and deserve. The provision of high quality goods and services begins with the recruitment process.

(Schuler, Randalls, 1989) explained recruitment is as " the set of activities and processes used to legally obtain a sufficient number of qualified applicants at the right place and time. So that the applicants and the organization can select each other in their own best short and long term interests. Thus, it seems that successful recuritment begins with proper employment planning and forecasting. So any one organization needs analyze what kinds of positions of future needs talent available within and outside of the organization and the current and anticipated resources that can be expected to attract and retain such talent. Thus, HR manager needs have one successful strategy to be prepared to employ in order to identify and select the best candidates for its developing pool of human resources.

In common, one successful recuruitment strategy involves these several processes of :

Step one : Development of a policy on recruitment and giving life to the policy.

Step two: Needing assessment to determine the current and future human resource requirement of the organization.

Step three: If the activity is to be effective , the HR requirements for each job category and functional division /unit of the organization must be assessed, identification within and outside the organization of the potential human resources pool.

Step four: Job analysis and job evaluation to identify the individual aspects of each jobs and calculate its relative worth, assessment of qualifications profiles, job descriptions that identify responsibilities and requirement skills, abilities , knowledge and experience, determination to pay salaries and benefits within a defined period.

Step five: identification and documentation of the actual process of recruitment and selection to ensure equity and laws.

Thus, the psychological recruitment strategy for the interviewer includes how to ask interview questions, how to give interview scores and panellists' comments, results of tests (where administered). Because and length of interview time for the interview. There are any interview main contents to any interviewer needs to concern how to arrange interview process. For example, nowadays, it is popular internet recruiting. Although, interviewer can reduce time to arrange and spend time to interview any applicants, due to the interviewer can interview any applicants from whose organization website . Specially, there are many similar potential interview competitors to apply to the position at the same time. Otherwise, internet recruiting is not all positive. Such as some applicants skill place great value in face-to-face interactons in the hiring process. Such applicant;s are likely to ignre jobs posted, impersonally on time.

I shall indicate these sample recruitment strategy to explain how to influence every applicant's choice to apply the job or not apply the job as below:

The first is online recruiting. This online recuritment strategy has a large percentage of employees are hired by human service agencies for every level jobs are seeking their first career job. The newspaper want ads are not an effective recruitment source for most of today's applicants. Placing vacancy announcements online is more effective and economical than using most traditional forms of advertising. However, online recruitment is designed to close this gap: Not reaching majority of applicants, especially young graduates.

The second is campus recruiting and job fairs. This campus recruiting strategy attracts both professional and paraprofessional applicants, who can be effectively recruited at job fairs sponsored by state workforce development agencies. However, college recruiting can be a very effective method for attracting applicants for professional jobs. The possible psychological advantages to applicants that includes any employers will send team of HR representatives to any colleges to provide an opportunity for job seekers to ask both job specific and hiring process/benefits questions; sending an ambassador to classrooms to quest lecture; schedule experienced employees or supervisors to ask on a hot topic in the human or service field at a local college or university. However, this campus recruiting strategy has a large percentage of employees hired, but need to improve overall applicant.

The third is university partner developing a variety of recruitment strategy. University partnership benefits include to collaborate with university deans and professors to help student interest in the field as well as to develop program partially covering college tuition and other expenses of college students who agree to work for the human service agency for specified periods of time. Its recruitment strategy aims to develop a variety of recruitment strategies with area universities, community colleges and schools of social work to encourage students to pursue careers in the human services. It's weakness lacks enough applicants with specialized social work degrees.

The fourth recruitment strategy is target recruitment. Employers may used a more diverse workforce that better reflects the client population who serve. For example, employers may need to recruit employees with specific lannguage skills or with specialized degrees , e.g. criminal juice. It' weakness lacks of diversity in targeted jobs.

The fifth recruitment strategy is internships. Interns sometimes are paid stipend, but in most instances interns are fulfilling an academic requirement of the college or university. Although supervisors and/or cause work staff must spend time supervising and training interns, the potential payoff is having a known applicant who is familiar with agency operations. Its weakness is needed to improve overall applicant pool.

The sixth recruitment strategy is maintain a pre-screened applicant pool. It has a pool of pre-screened, interviewed applicants always available to be called for a second interview with the hiring supervisor. When, using this approach, it's important to minimize the amount of time between the initial interview and the second interview to prevent top quality applicants from being hired human resources will need to do continuous recruiting and screening , even when there are no current vacancies. It's weaknesses include that some

human services organizations delay hiring until staff vacancies reach crisis proportions. They than initiate a recruitment process that is designed to bring new employees on board as soon as possible . The unfortunate result is hiring employees who meet the minimum requirements, but nothing more. It also has too many applicants get hired with only the minimum credentials.

The seventh recruitment strategy is realistic job previews. Realistic job previews are designed to prevent applicants from taking jobs that who have life knowledge of or are not suited to perform. It is a recruiting tool is designed to reduce early turnover by communicating both the desirable and the undesirable aspects of a jobs before applicants accept a job offer. It can be in the form of videos, oral presentations, job shadowing opportunities. It's weakness includes unwanted turnover among new workers who did not understand their job when who were hired.

The final recruitment strategy is improved hiring flexibilities in highly centralized systems. It means many public-seator human service agencies are regulated by merit systems that make it different to attract and maintain the interest of top-qualify applicants. Top applicants in today's economy are searching the interest for jobs that are available now. They aren't interested in taking a civil service exam and sitting on eligibility lists for months. In some systems requirements and lengthy inflexible scoring processes wash out well qualified applicants. It's weaknesses include hiring process takes too long, high qualify applicants are looking elsewhere for jobs.

● How to apply occupational psychological
test method to test applicant's ability?

Occupational psychological interview method is the application of the science of psychology to test applicant individual work ability. For example, any interviews can apply occupational psychologists' test method to attempt to test applicant individual performance, motivation and wellbing of the organization in the workplace. If any interviewers can attempt to apply occupational psychologist test method to test any applicant individual working abilities in interview. It brings this question: How can the interviewer develop, apply and evaluate a range of tools and interventions to test the applicant individual working abilities across many different areas of the workplace?

The occupational psychological test method can include these psychological skills to test every applicant individual ability in interview. Such as : Psychological assessment means selecting and assessing the applicant individual ability using interview enquiring method, e.g. in interview, enquiring applicant concerns on how to solve crisis deal issues when challenges cause in any workplace, assessments of what the applicant's main ability centres are. Situational judgement tests, e.g. how to solve challenges in different situations and personality questionnaires and cognitive ability tests. Profiling jobs are matching requirements to the applicant's future performance. Developing and choosing is valid, reliable, fair and suitable selectin procedures.

Thus, the psychological enquiring questions can concern on work motivation, performance, appraisal and management, leadership power influence and negotiation, employee engagement and commitment, citizenship and positive behaviors or counterproductive in workplace, psychology of group teams and teamwork different aspects, which have similar points , such as concern organizational behavior questions. It aims to test the applicant how to deal any immediate crisis in the organization if the interviewer decides to employ him/her.

The key focus of how to achieve one effective psychological test to the applicant in the interiew. It focuses on key areas , such as the applicant personal goal attainment, interview performance, the applicnt's mind on innovation and creativity aspects, and well being in the workplace how the applicant explains who will perform supposes who did the job in the workplace.

In the interview, the interviewer needs the applicant to

explain to let him/her to understand how the applicant's relation and motivation in the organization. The interviewer also needs to know how the applicant can solve any challenges in workplace in the suitation test interview. Because conflict resolution is a challenging environment to work in. However, any downsides are offset by the rewards of being able to help protect both the organization and its employees from the psychological , physiological and economic costs of conflict. Because conflict will occur in possible in any workplaces. Thus, the interviewer ought to ask the question to let him/her to know the applicant will solve if who did this position.

Human factors is a discipline concerned with how the successful interview applicant (future employee) works effectively and safely. It considers a employee's environmental , organizational, job and individual characteristics. These factors will affect the organizational successful interview applicant (future employee) behavior and it is past of the interviewer's job to analyze these and to give recommendations for change to improve human performance to the organization if who selected to employ these applicants in every time interview. Thus it seems occupational psychological test method can give benefits to the interviewer to understand more to the applicants to judge whether who will be the most suitable applicant(s)to do any positions in whose organization more accurate decision in any interviews.

THREE

SELECTING AND EVALUATING ASSESSMENT METHODS

How selection assessment methods are applied to choose the best applicants ? Organizations compete in the war for talent. So, one effective selection assessment method can help any organizations to choose the best applicant(s). Using scientifically proven assessments to make selection decisions, even though such assessments have been shown to result in significant productivity increases, cost savings, decrease other critical organizational outcomes. I shall indicate common misconceptions about selection tests, such as: Screening applicants for conscientiousness will yield better performers , then screening applicants for intelligence, screening applicants for their values will yield better performers , then screening applicants for intelligence, integrity tests are not ueful because job candidates misrepresent themselves on these typs of tests, unstructured interviews with candidates provide better information than structured assessment processes and using selection tests creates legal problems for organizations rather than helps to solve them.

There are numerous different types of formal assessments that organizations can use to select employees. The first step in developing or selecting an assessment method for a given situation is to understand what the job requires employees to do and what knowledge, skills and abilities individuals must posses in order to perform the job effectively. This is typically accomplished by conducting a job analysis . For job oriented job analysis recruitment example, providing test by stating fact and answer questions, gathering and reviewing information to obtain obtain evidence or develop background information on subjects, integrating diverse information to uncover relationships between individuals, events or evidences.

Other assessment methods focus on how measuring the best applicant who are required to perform job tasks effectively, such as various mental abilities, physical abilities or personality traits, depending on the job's requirements. If one were to assess whether candidates could solve decisive and communicate effectively. Alternatively, if one were selecting an administrative assistant, such as the ability to perform work conscientiously with speed and accuracy would be such more important for identifying capable candidates. Some worker-oriented or job analysis data are used as a basis for developing assessment method, that focus on a job candidate's underlying abilities to perform important work task.

In general, any organization interviews only divide either internal or external both selection. Internal selection refers to situations where organization is hiring or promoting from within, whereas, external selection refers to situations where an organization is hiring from the outside. When some assessent methods are used more commonly for external selection. (e.g. cognitive ability tests, personality tests, integrity tests). There are numerous examples of organizations that have used one or more of the following tools for internal selection, external selection or both. I shall explain what the differences for these interview test methods as follow:

What is cognitive ability tests. These assessment measure a variety of mental abilities, such as verbal and mathematical ability, reasoning ability and reading comprehension. Cognitive ability tests have been shown to be extremely useful predictors of job performance and thus are used frequently in making selection decisions for many different types of jobs (Hunter, J. 1986, Ree, M.J. & Teachout, M.S. 1984, Gottredson, L.S. 1982).

Cognitive ability tests typically consist of multipler choice items that are administered via a paper-and-pencil instructment or computer. Some cognitive ability tests contain test items that need various abilities, e.g. verbal ability, numberical ability etc. But then sum up the correct answers to all of the items to obtain a singl total score. The total score then represents a measure of general mental ability. If a separate score is computed for each of the specific types of abilities, then the resulting scores represent measures of the specific mental abilities.

Job knowledge tests mean these assessments measure critical knowledge areas that are needed to perform a job effectively. Typically, the knowledg areas measured represent technical knowledge. Job knowledge tests are used in situations m where candidates must clearly possess a body of knowledge prior to job entry. Job knowledge tests are not appropriate to use in situations where candidates will be trained after selection on the on knowledge areas who need to have. Like cognitive ability tests, job knowledge tests typically consist of multiple-choice items administered via a paper-and-pencil instrument or a computer , although essay items are sometimes included in job knowledg tests (Hunter, J. 1986).

Personality tests that assess traits relevant to job performance have been shown to be effective predictors of subsequent job performance. The personality factors that are assessed most frequently in work situations include conscientiousness, extraversion, agreeableness, openness to experience and emotional stability (Barrick, M.R. & Mount, M.K. 1991, Costa, P.T. Jr., & Mccae, r. R. 1982).

Research has shown that conscientiousness is the most useful predictor of performance across many different jobs. Although some of the other pesonality factors have been shown to be useful predictors of peformance in specific types of jobs (Hough, L.M. 1992). It can consist of several multipe choice or true/false items measuring each personality factor. Like cognitive ability and knowledge tests, which are also administered in a paper-and-pencil or computer format.

Biographical data (biodata) inventories, which ask job candidates questions covering their background, personal characteristics or interests have been shown to be effective predictors of job performance (Stokes, G.S. & Owens, W.A. 1994, Shoenfeldt, L.F. 1999). Another form of a biodata inventory is an instrument called an " accomplishment stored". With this types of assessment, candidates prepare a written account of their most meritorious accomplishments in key skill and ability areas that are required for a job , e.g. planning and organizing, customer service, conflict resolution (Hough, L.M. 1984).

Integrity tests measure attitudes and experiences that are related to an individual honesty, trustworthiness and dependability (Sackett, P.R. & Wanek, J.E. 1996). It is typically multiple-choice in format and administered via a paper-and-pencil instrument or a computer.

Physical fitness tests are used in some selection situations. These tests require candidates to perform general physical activities to assess one's overall fitness, strength or other physical capabilities necessary to perform the job.

Situational judgement tests provide job candidates with situations that who would encounter on the job and viable options for handling the presented situations (Mecichmann, D., Schmitt, N. & Harvey, V.S. 2001). depending on how the test is designed , candidates are asked to select the most effective or most and least effective ways of handling the situaton from the response options provided. Situational judgement tests are more complicated to develop than many of the other types of assessments. It is because more difficulty in developing scenarios with several likely response options that are all viable, but in fact, some are reliably rated as being more effective than others. Situational judgement tests are typically administered in written or paper-and-pencil test booklet or on a computer.

Assessment centers are a type of work sample test that is typically focused on assessing higher-level managerial and supervisory competencies (Thornton, G.C III 1992). Assessment centers usually last at least a day and up to several days. They typically include role-play exercises in -basket exercises, analytical exercises and group discussion exercises. Trained assessors observe the performane of candidates during the assessment process and evaluate them on standardized rating. Some assessment centers also include other types of assessment methods, such as cognitive ability, job knowledge and personality tests. It should be noted selection purposes that assessment centers aren't only used for comprehensive development feedback to participants.

Physical ability tests are used regularly to select workers for physiclly demanding jobs, such as police officers and firefighters. These test are similar to work sample tests in that who typically require candidates to perform a series of actual job tasks to determine whether or not who can perform the physical requirements of a jobs. Physical ability tests are often scored in a pass/fail basis. To pass, the complete set of taks that comprise the test must be properly completed within a specified timeframe.

● How to criteria for selecting and evaluating assessment methods in interview?

Properly identifying and implementing formed assessment methods to select employees is one of the more complex areas for HR department to learn about and understand. This is because understanding selection testing requires knowledge of statistics, measurement issues and legal issues relevant to testing.

I recommend any interviewers need to understand important criteria to decide to choose which kind of interview test is the suitable to test applicant individual abilities in every interview such as below:

The first criteria includes validity. Validity means the extent to which the assessment method is useful for predicting subsequent job performance. Adverse impact means the extent to which protected group members , e.g. minorities, females and individualds over 40 score lower on the assessment than majority group members.

The second criteria includes cost. Cost is both to develop and to administer the assessment. Applicant reactions means the extent to which applicants react positively versus negtively to the assessment method. For example, cognitive ability test. on the positive side, this type of assessment is high on validity and low on costs. However, it is also high on adverse impact, moderately favorable. Thus, when cognitive tests are inexpensive and very useful for predicting subsequent job performance, minoritie score significantly lower on them than whites. There is no simple, formulaic approach for selecting " one best" assessment method, because all of them have advantages and disadvantages.

However, the most important consideration in evaluating on assessment method is its validity. Validity refers to whether or not the assessment method provides useful information about how effectively an employee will actually perform once who is hired for a job. Validity is the most important factor in considerating whether or not to use an assessment method because identify who will doesn't accurately identify who will perform effectively on a job has no value to the organization.

There are two major forms of validity: criterion-related validity and content validity is a simple example will illustrate how criterion-related validity can be established. Assume that a sales job requires employees to have a high level of customer service orientation and an organization decides to implement a selection test that assesses prospective applicants on their customer service skills. In order to show that the client skills assessment is a valid predictor of peformance , it must be shown that individuals who score higher on the assessment perform better. On the job and individuals who score lower on the assessment perform less well on the job. Thus, validity in this case would be defined as a meaningful relationship between how well people performed on the assessment and how well who subsequently performed on the job. Content validity approach to validation involves demonstrating that an assessment provides a direct measure of how well candidates will actually perform to job. This type of validation requires analyzing the job to identify the tasks that are performed.

What are the differences between criterion related versus content validation. Criterion-related validity can be used to evaluate the validity of any assessment where individuals receive scores that reflect how well who perform on the test and these scores are subsequently shown to relate to how well who perform on the job. Content validation can only be used to validate assessments that provide a direct measure of how well candidates perform job tasks or the content of the jobs, such as work sample tests. Otherwise, criterion-related validity evidence or contect validity . Thus, it is more desirable to obtain if it is possible to conduct a successful unbiased performance measures must be available. Unfortunately, performance appraisal ratings, which are the most commonly used performance measures can be inaccurate and often fail.

Adverse impact is examined by comparing the proportion of majority group who are selected from a job to the protected group members who are selected. When organizations are and should be interested in selecting the higher quality work force possible, many are also concerned about selecting a diverse workforce ought not using measures that will systematically produce adverse impact against protected groups.

In conclusion, either if an assessment method is shown to produce adverse impact and the organization wished to continue the last of that assessment, there are legal requirements to ensure that the method must have demonstrated validity or if an organization uses an assessment that produces adverse impact that produces adverse impact without the validity evidence. The organization will encounter challenges against which it won't be able to prevail. When evidence of validity can be used to justify and defend the use of measures that produce an adverse impact many organizations nonetheless attempt to apply the adverse impact produced be their assessment methods to extent possible in order to minimize potential interview wrong recuritment decisions and lack of diversity concerns issues to recruit any the most suitable applicants to do any positions in any organizations.

Reference

Barrick, M. R. & Mount , M.K. (1991). The big five personality dimensions and job performance: A meta-analysis, personnel psychology, 91, 1-26.

Costa, P.T. & Jr., & McCrae, R.R. (1992). Four ways five factors are basic. Personality and individual differences, 13, 653-665.

Gottredson, L.S. (Ed). (1982). The g factor in employment, Journal of vacational behavior, 29(3).

Hough, L.. (1992) The big five personality variables construct confusion: Description versus prediction human performance, 5, 135-155.

Hough, L.M. (1984). Development and evaluation of the " accomplishment record" methods of selecting and promoting professonals. Journal of applied psychology, 69, 135-146.

Hunter, J. (1986). Cognitive ability, cognitive aptitudes, job knowledge and job performance, Journal of vacational behavior, 29, 340-362.

Meichmann, D., Schmitt, N., & Harvey, V.S. (20010. Incremental validity of situatinal judgement tests , Journal of applied psychology, 86, 410-417.

Ree, M.J. Earles, J.A., & Teachout, M.S. (1994), Predicting job performance: Hot much more than g. Journal of applied psychology, 79, 518-524.

Robserton, I. T., & Smith, M. (2001). Personnel Selection. Journal Of Occupational And Organizational Psychological Psychology, 74(4), 441-472.

Sackett, P.R. & Wanek, J.E. (1996). New developments in the use of measures of honesty, integrity, conscientiousness, dependability, trustworthiness and reliability for personnel selection, personnel psychology, 49, 787-829.

Schuler, Randalls, S: Personnel and human resources management. Third edition, 1987.

Shoenfeldt, L.F. (1999). From dustbowl empiricism to rational constructs in biodata. Human resource management review, 9, 147-167.

Steven, Kay Cynthia (1997). Effects of pre-interview beliefs on applicant's reactions to campus interviews. Academy of management journal, 40(4), 947-966.

Stokes, G.S. Mumford, M.D. & owen, W.A. (Eds.) (1994). Biodata handbook paloacto, CA: CPP Books.

Thornton, G.C. III (1992). Assessment centers in human resources management Addison-Wesley,

Whetton, D.A. & Cameron, K.S. (2002). Developing Management , Skill 5th edition, reading, MA: Addison Wesley Longman.

FOUR

LEARNING HOW TO RESEARCH QUALITATIVE INTERVIEW SKILL

In human resource department, human resource manager and interviewers need to interview the applicatns when they apply the different positions to work in their organizations. How to achieve efficient and effective interviews to achieve the most eight applicant choice in short time and to avoid lot of time and human resource expenditure spending. So, managers need to learn how to achieve qualitative interview methods in order to avoid any non essential waste for every interview.

In fact, different forms of interview serve different purposes, e.g. journalistic interviews are means of recording and reporting important events in society , therapeutic interviews seel to improve debilitating siutations in people's lives and research interviews have the purpose of producing knowledge . However, these are not necessarily hard and fast distinctions between these interview forms for qualitative research and interviews sometimes come close to journalistic interviews and some qualitative researchers attempt their interview practice as a learning process of changes in the interviewees' or applicants' lives in the interview process.

I shall indicate different interviewing questins for different positions to let the interviewer can ask the more suitable questions to test every applicant's personal problem solving ability in order to evaluate whom is the most right applicant to do the position in the organization as below:

For any management position application example, the suitation interview method is the most suitable interview method. When many applicants apply the manager position in the school organizatiom, the interviewer can attempt to ask these questions to evaluate every one's managerial solving ability when every encounters any problems to need to deal their tasks daily. The interview questions may include: Do you think that's good? When you are encouraged more from your same level staffs and they want you manage teacher team in our school?

When the management position applicant listens the interviewer's these two questions. They will begin to plan hoe to answer these questions immediately in ten seconds . Because this kind of management position application interiew usually many only allow ten to twenty minutes limited time. So, if the interviewee (applicant) can answer to these questions immediately. Then, the interviewer can ask another suitation question immediately.. So, it means that the applicant (interviewee) can have more chance to let him/her to answer more different situational problems if he/she can spend little time to mind every question. Then, the interviewer can follow his/her different opinions how to answet the situational problems to make more rational evaluation to the applicant's managerial ability level.

So, such as above question, some applicants will need to spend more time to mind how to answer this question. It is possible that they had not encountered this suitation in their past working careers. Otherwise, some applicants won't need to spend more time to mind how to answer this question. It is possible that they had encountered this suitation in their past working careers. However, their answers won't absolute same because every applicant has different educational level , daily living experience, working experience in their past. So, they will apply themselves educational knowledge, past working experience and daily living experience to answer this question, It is one subjective of personal feeling question , it concerns what the feeling to the applicant when this school has many same level staffs appreciate he/she has managerial effort to manage this school's teachers team.

Moreover, some applicants may feel they have little managerial experience. So, they will give a negative emotion answer , such as: I feel my same level staffs allow for the creativity of my individual managerial ability to modify the program and to promote me to manage this school's teachers team. But, if they want everything lock stepped, identical no. I think it would be disastrous and different, because they have going to get some people that won't think at all, that just not back and coast on somebody else's brains, and I don't feel that's good for anybody.

Then, the interviewer can ask this question: Do you feel you've given that spce at the moment? Then, some managerial position applicants (interviewees) usually give these similar answers, such as: with my teaching partner, I am. I know with some others here, I wouldn't be, even I should go crazy. Usually, the lacking managerial experience applicants will spend little time to answer this question, because they feel lack actual enough managerial experience in past schools to lead and they can not find some reasons to explain whether they have what strengths or efforts to manage this school teaches team and whether they ought how to manage this school's teachers team to raise their teaching performance effectively.

Then, the interviewer can ask this question: How would that be ..... Some owning more confident applicants will indicate some useful main points ot methods to solve how to manage teachers problems. Some owning less confident applicants won't indicate some useful main points or methods to solve how to manage teachers team problems. So , these suitational interview questions, it can reflect whether he/she has encountered any managerial problems to be needed to solve in their past education career. However, these are more average applicants choose to answer this question, they will apply time arrangement or time management method to attempt any teachers management problems. These general applicants may answer this similar style answer, such as: Basically controlled, first of all it would be their ideas, it is not myself idea to promote or appreciate myself to do this teacher member manager position and if I do this position, I would have to fit into their teaching style , and it would have to fit into their time arrangement or time management in order to let me can cooperate to do teaching tasks more easily and efficiently. However, I think that I shall feel this managerial problem is that there are no any teachers should have to work like that.

So, it is general sommon answers , many teachers team mangerial leader applicants will only concerns time arrangement problem. So, this time arrangement problem answer group applicants, their managerial problem efforts ought be common generally. If one applicant can identify other managerial problems and recommend the useful opinions to solve the other discovered problems. Clearly, then the applicant will be possible the most right applicant to do this teacher team managerial leader in the school. So , when the school has many applicants , e.g. more than fifty , even one hundred . Also, if the interviewer needs o spend the weak at least interviewing time to interview every in order to evaluate whether whom has more managerial effort to solve any teacher team task problem daily. This kind of situational interviewing questions soluable method will be one effective optional test method in order to make the more accurate right applicant choice.

However, it is possible that there are none of right applicant to do this teacher team managerial leader position from external recruitment. If this school can not find one owning school managerial effort applicant to do this position. Then, it ought find whom has teacher team managerial experience from its internal organizational promotion choice in its school organization.

In conclusion, situational problem solution interviewing method can be applied to any managerial position application in any organizations, for internal interview or external interview recruitment choices. The interviewer can evaluate whether whom applicant has more managerial effort when interviewer asks any kinds of situational problem questions and he/she listens their different opinions in the limited interviewing time in order to compare whose answers are more reasonable or rational to identify whose managerial effort to satisfy his /her organizational managerial problem needs. So, interviewers need to learn whether they ought ask which kinds of situational questions to enquire every applicant , when they apply the position. Because every applicant's educational level, working experience, living experience and age is different. The interviewer ought follow every applicant's unique characteristics to ask different situational questions. For example, if the applicant lacks managerial experience to manage one car company salespeople team, he/she has car company marketing advertisemen team managerial experience only. But, the interviewer only consider to enquire whether how he/she can manage the car company's salespeople team to raise ccar sale skill in short time before. Moreover, the applicant knows how to apply the suitable advertisement methods to attract car buyers' choices to his/her company's different styles of cars. It will cause the applicant feels difficult to answer the car sale situational problem. It is one unfair and not suitable situational problem to ask the applicant, when he.she needs to spend little time to mind how to answer the situational problem in the interview between the car company's CEO and the interviewee.

In conclusion, in any managerial position application interview, every interviewer needs to review eery applicant's educational backgroung, working experience and living experience and age in order to arrange the most suitable situational problems to ask them to achieve the most fair, reasonable , rational interview choice method.

Psychological interview methods

FIVE

INTERVIEW PSYCHOLOGY METHODS

In human resource department, interviewing and selecting the most right applicants to do different kinds of positions, it is one part of HRM function. If the interviewer need to spend more time to interview to decide whom is the most right applicant to do the position in one day, e.g. 50 at least , even more applicants number as well as he/she can also make the more accurate personal selection decision to choose the most right applicant to do the position after the interview day. Then, the interviewing process needs to be avoided to spend more time to choose the most suitable applicant to do the position within the day. It is difficult to judge whether whom ought be the most right applicant to do the position, if there are more than 50 applicants , they are needed to be interview in the day. The consequence will bring HR department can spend extra time to do the interview task, but it can have enough staffs and time and resource to do other urgent or important task at the interview day. It will bring this question: How to apply psychological method to raise interviewer's efficiency to shorten to spend extra time to do interviewing tasks ? I shall explain some psychological methods to attempt to let interviewers have more confidence to select the most right applicant in short time as below:

1. Behavioral interview skill

The interviewer can apply the actual behavioral interview method to let the interviewee to answer how he/she deals the matters, he/she feels that it is the best decision in order to judge and analyze whether whom applicant is the most suitable to be selected, e.g. describing the situation, he/she needs or the task that he/she needs to accomplish. The situation may be from a previous job, any relevant event, describing the action he/she took and be sure to keep the focus on him/her , e.g. discussing a group project or effort in the team; explaining what results he/she achieved, what happen? How did the event and what dis the applicant a ccomplishes? What did the applicant learn?

In the behavioral-based interview. the interviewer can need the applicant to attempt to explain examples clearly in order to judge whose analytical skill whether he/she is the suitable applicant to do the position. The interviewer may ask the applicant to identify some examples from whose post experience where he/she demonstrated top behaviors and skills that employers typically seek. To judge whether his/her examples should be totally positive, such as accomplishments or meeting goals, the other half should be situations that started at negatively , but either ended positively or he/she made the best of the outcome.

This behavioral interview test aims to review whether the applicant's every example answer, he/she can provide an appropriate description of how he/she demonstrated the desired behaviors. In the behavioral interview, the interviewer can attempt to judge whether the applicant has good imagine effort to mind any relatively small set of examples to respond to a number of different behavioral questions to satisfy the right example are applied to the right situations in the limited interview time. Hence, behavioral interview can let the interviewer to make more accurate analysis to judge whether whom applicant(s) has (have) good analytical effort to solve any work-related situational problems in the most reasonable way or attitude in order to select whom is the most right applicant to do the position.

2. E-mail interviewing in qualitative research

E-mail interviewing is another good interview method to select right applicant to do the managerial level position. E-mail interviewing can be in many cases a viable alternative to face-to-face telephone interviewing. Internet-based qualitative research methods may include online personal interview and virtual focus groups. However, it brings two questions: What opportunities and challenges does online in depth interviewing present for collectively qualitative data? How can in depth e-mail interviews be conducted effectively?

The applicant targets may be the top-level manager, advertising executive , sales manager, human resource manager etc. management position applicants. They need to answer any complex or difficult interviewing question by email in the limited time, e.g. how to solve one case study problem , how to give recommendation to solve the situation problem. The interview participants may be recruited by tool/method of psychological test questions, the interview questions may be interview guide in a single e-mail and follow yp, length of email data collection period may be up to 10 weeks, the number of e-mail or follow up exchanges may be several number. The electronic formal and require little editing or formation before the applicants are processed for analysis all e-mail interviewing questions. So, they need to answer any managerial case study problem in limited time.

It is one good managerial interview test method to evaluate whether whom applicant has the best analysis effort in order to the managerial position, because they need to find the best solutions to give recommendations to attempt to solve any situational problems in any un predictive case study problems. For example, when the applicant or a focus group of discussion applicants whom need to spend the maximum half hours to give recommendations to discuss to solve one complex or difficult case study problem either between the interviewer and the another interviewee applicant or between the group of five to ten interviewees (job applicants) themselves. Thus, after the interviewer sent the one case study question to let the applicants to know by every email channel. The interviewer needs to judger whether whom one applicant or one of the focus group applicants their recommendations are the most reasonable to solve the case study managerial situational problem within half hour to one hour. Then, the interviewer can make more accurate judgement to select whether whom has the best analytical effort to do the managerial position.

3. The effectiveness of motivational interviewing for young or older adult applicants selection process

How can apply case management skills to be effective to prepare any interview motivation? How to do the most effective and efficient to meet the objectives of the interview? Some interview techniques used may vary the

based on the individuals involved in the interview. For an interview with the young age applicant more require a different approach than an interview with a senior adult applicant. The following are one pointers to assist with preparing for the interview as below:
Knowing the purpose of the interview and what needs to be accomplished . What is the expected outcome? Gathering all forms that need to be completed or signed having the interview and making list of questions that need to be asked, knowing the key facts and topics to be discussed, during the interview. Gathering factual information that may be helpful. Opening mind is needed in the whole interview process. Making an appointment for the interview and arranging sufficient time to set fully participate in the interview. Taking notes during the interview, let the participants know in general terms the reason notes are being made and how they will be used, opening ended questions invite the applicant to provide more information usually begin with other words who, what, where, how, asking one question at a time and keeping wording simple and specific, defining any terms that may be unfamiliar to the applicant , giving the interviewing participants in the interview an opportunity to ask their one questions or to clarify anything that was discussed, closing the interview with a review of the information discussed and facts gathered, reviewing any follow-up that is to be done by the case manager or others involved in the interview.

In an efficient and effective interview, the interviewer needs have good body and spoken word communication to the interviewee or the position applicant. Because a good communication can reduce waste time or avoid the extended longer interview time if the interviewer can make good communication to impact good message to let the applicant to understand what is the mean to his/her interview question. What he/she wants to know, the total impact of a message includes ,e.g. 7 % verbal (words), 38% vocal /volume, pitch, rhythm etc. and 55% body movements (mostly facial expression). The interviewer's body and verbal behavior can make more clear message to let the interviewee(job applicant) to understand what answers are he/she wants to know mostly. Hence, an efficient and effective interview can let the interviewer to control and manage the whole interview to evaluate whether whom the applicants' answers or feedbacks are more reasonable to be acceptable to be better to compare other applicants to apply the position more accurately.

- What are common psychology methods of recruitment choice?

Can any psychology methods are used to choose who will be the best recruitment applicant(s) in any recruitment stage more accurate? Can the interviewer observe the applicant's psychological phenomenon to judge whether the applicant can be the best or the most suitable applicant in the recruitment stage more accurate? To answer above these questions. We need to know why a systematic scientific procedure is an essential component to achieve any psychological method(s) to test candidate individual ability to judge whether who is the best or the
most suitable applicant to do any position in any organization.

A psychologist can follow a systematic scientific procedure which has theoretical base in order to explain and interpret the psychological phenomenon of the applicant to decide whether who is the best or the most suitable applicant to do the position in the organization.

On the one hand, in order to obtain the applicant's psychological response from individual applicant, there are a number of psychological tools or instruments are used during the interview process. The responses are taken on these tools constitute the basic data which are analyzed to study the applicant experiences, e.g. working experiences, life experiences, mental processes and behaviors. On the other hand, in order to understand every applicant's behavior during the interview process. The different psychological methods can be applied for solving different applicant's individual behavior (individual mental problems) to judge who will be the best or the most suitable applicant to the position in any organization. Because different situations will cause the applicant to choose how to do or perform different behaviors to persuade the interviewer believes who is the best or the most suitable applicant to do the position in the organization. Thus, whose performances will be shaped by many factors both intrinsic and extrinsic to him or her in any interview process.

The common psychological methods of interview process include such as: For observation psychological method example, when shopping in the market , the researcher must have noticed various activities of the consumers . When he/she observes the consumers their activities, the researcher also think about as to why who are doing those activities and probably the researcher reaches a conclusion about the causes of such activities. So, observation is as a psychological method of enquiry is often understand as a systematic registering of events without any deliberate attempt to interface with variables operating in the event which is being studies.

Thus, observation psychological method seems to be applied to judge who is the best or the most suitable applicant to do any position in any organization in any interview process. Such as in any interview process, the interviewer (observer) can use this method to judge or observe every applicant's face and behavioral performance to feel whether who is the best or the most suitable applicant who own ability or confidence or qualification or experience to already to do the job to achieve the recruitment result is more accurate. For example, the interviewer (observer) can attempt to give one simple or difficult task to test whether whom the applicant has the more effort of the induced stress on task performance in the short time observation test in the on part stage of the interview process.

However, observation is also divided into either participant or non-participant both types, depending on the role of observer (interviewer). In the case of interview participant observation, the interviewer mixes up with the job (task) performance event test under study and conducts concerns the interview test, e.g. group discussion interview test, the applicants and the interviewer will discuss one or more than one topic(s) which concern(s) on relating the position requirement issue. So, the interviewer can analyze whom applicant(s) can talk the most reasonable evidences to support whose opinions to argue the topic against the other applicants together among of them in the short time group discussion, e.g. between 15 minutes to 30 minutes. It aims to let the interviewer can have enough time to record whose opinions to analyze whose opinions are the most reasonable argument to support whose main points to win this position among these interview competitors in the short time group discussion. Thus, the interviewer needs to participate the group discussion to ask every applicant any questions and let them to attempt to solve any challenges in the whole group discussion. After the group discussion, then the interviewer can have more effort or confidence to judge whom applicant (s) is/are the most suitable or the best applicant (s) to do the job for his/her organization more accurate.

Otherwise, as in the case of interview non-participant observation, the interviewer maintains an optimum distance and has little impact on the interview event. Such as the interview group discussion test. The interviewer won't ask any questions to let the applicants to attempt to answer. Otherwise, he/she will let the applicants have chance to ask any questions or answer the questions among of their discussion related to the topic. So the interviewer's role is a listener, who only needs to listen every applicant how who can ask and can answer any questions to decide who can talk the most correct or the right or the most reasonable answers to answer their questions in the short time group discussion. Then, the interviewer can record all applicants' questions and answers to make the judgement to decide who will be the right or the most suitable applicant to do the position in her/him organization more accurate.

- Why does need to test the applicant's psychological behavior in the interview process?

To answer this question, we need to know why any large or middle size organizations which need have human resource department. To challenge of today's HR managers is to create a pool of good employees in the organization. It starts from selection process of the employees. So, interview has been used as an important selection method by HR managers for long time. The cost of rehiring the importance of hiring the right person for right position first. It requires a reliable and valid interview process. Although, any interview won't guarantee 100 percent success in hiring the best employees into any organization, but the proper application is at least, will improve the chances of hiring the best applicant for the job the organization. The importance is given to the selection of right employees for the right positions. Firms are now realizing the value of the good employees because who can make a difference through their job performance. So, various selection methods are now being used to identify the right candidate.

" Interview" has emerged as a very useful tool in this regard. It is a very common selection method and has a high predictive validity for job performance (Robertson, & Smith , 2001). The main purpose of the interview is to select the right candidate for the right job. The importance of conducting an effective interview is also rising. So consensus was found among the HR experts regarding the effective interview techniques. There are a number of existing literatures regarding the techniques of an effective interview, but every few literatures exist regarding a systematic approach of conducting exist regarding a systematic approach of conducting an effective interview.

This is a very few literatures exist regarding a complete interview process that shows a clear path to the employers for selecting right employees. A lot of interview technique are available, but the problem arises regarding the use of these techniques in a concrete manner. A systematic approach of interview will facilitate the tasks of HR managers in selecting the right applicant for the right position.

(Stevens, 1997) author indicated the whole process of the interview has been described in terms of "3D"- Development, discussion and decision. This study is particularly important for three reasons. First , it will help the HR mangers to think about the employee selection interview in a concrete manner. Second, it will help them to use a number of interview techniques in an effective way that will ultimately increase the chance of hiring the right person for the right position. Third, it will enrich the existing literature of selection interview.

(Stevens, 1997) author also explained that the growing importance of good employees will cause a challenge to the HR managers. The selection process of today's HR manager is becoming complex and challenging. Undoubtedly, the overall aim, of the selection process is to identify the candidates who are suitable for the vacancy or wider requirement of the HR plan. " Interview" has been used as a ' critical selection method ' by HR managers. The interview is the most valid method in determining an applicant's organizational fit, level of motivation and inter-personal selects.

Whetton & Cameron (2002) cited steps of process of conducting an interview, what they named as People-oriented selection interview process. Here is explains the interview process: P=prepare, E=establish rapport, O=obtain information, P=provide information, C= lead top close and E= evaluate.

So, it seems that the candidates' behavior individual performance in the interview process can be predicted whether who is(are) the most suitable or the best to do the position in the organization from the interviewer's observation. So, it also means the candidate's attitude in the interview process can perform to let the interviewer to feel whether who is suitable or the best to do the position in the organization . Thus, observation of the applicant individual performance, it is an interviewer's best interest to find good prospects, hire them and have them stay in the organization.

Therefore, the interviewees are needed to be provided sufficient information about the job and organization to have enough time to prepare before who will go to interview fairly. It aims to let every candidate has enough confidence to prepare to answer any questions in further interview process fairly. So, the development stage is a good preparation for the interview facilitates the effective interview process. To aim to let the candidate have enough preparation to interview , it should begin long before the first question is ever asked fairly.

In conclude, HR department seems an essential department to any middle or large organizations nowadays. It does not attribute only recruitment function to any organization, it also attribute the chance to give one psychological test function to evaluate whom applicant has the more experience and qualification and effort to do any position in any organization. If the interviewer has not prepared any psychological method to test any applicants to judge whether who has the more effort to do the position. Then, I believe the interview result will be more failure and more inaccurate to employ the most suitable applicant , due to who lacks the enough effort and qualification and experience to perform to finish any tasks or duties of the position . So, it is important why any organization needs have good psychological method to test and observe the applicant's psychological behavior in the interview process?

SIX

OCCUPATION PSYCHOLOGICAL TEST METHODS

How to apply psychological recruitment strategies effect to manage in the recruitment process? HR (human resource) managers understand accept that poor recruitment decisions continue to affect organizational performance and limit goal achievement. In this case, many jurisdictions to identify and implement new effective hiring strategies will be serious issue to any HR departments to concern.

Acquiring and retaining high-quality talent is critical to any organization's success. So, recruiters need to be more elective in their choice. Since poor recruiting decisions can produce long term negative effects, among their high training and development costs to minimize the incidence of poor performance and high turnover to impact staff morale, the production of high quality goods and services. Thus, HR managers must seek all possible methods for improve their output and provide the satisfaction to their clients require and deserve. The provision of high quality goods and services begins with the recruitment process.

(Schuler, Randalls, 1989) explained recruitment is as " the set of activities and processes used to legally obtain a sufficient number of qualified applicants at the right place and time. So that the applicants and the organization can select each other in their own best short and long term interests.

Thus, it seems that successful recruitment begins with proper employment planning and forecasting. So any one organization needs analyze what kinds of positions of future needs talent available within and outside of the organization and the current and anticipated resources that can be expected to attract and retain such talent. Thus, HR manager needs have one successful strategy to be prepared to employ in order to identify and select the best candidates for its developing pool of human resources.

In common, one successful recruuitment strategy involves these several processes of :

Step one : Development of a policy on recruitment and giving life to the policy.

Step two: Needing assessment to determine the current and future human resource requirement of the organization.

Step three: If the activity is to be effective , the HR requirements for each job category and functional division /unit of the organization must be assessed, identification within and outside the organization of the potential human resources pool.

Step four: Job analysis and job evaluation to identify the individual aspects of each jobs and calculate its relative worth, assessment of qualifications profiles, job descriptions that identify responsibilities and requirement skills, abilities , knowledge and experience, determination to pay salaries and benefits within a defined period.

Step five: identification and documentation of the actual process of recruitment and selection to ensure equity and laws.

Thus, the psychological recruitment strategy for the interviewer includes how to ask interview questions, how to give interview scores and panellists' comments, results of tests (where administered). Because and length of interview time for the interview. There are any interview main contents to any interviewer needs to concern how to arrange interview process.

For example, nowadays, it is popular internet recruiting. Although, interviewer can reduce time to arrange and spend time to interview any applicants, due to the interviewer can interview any applicants from whose organization website . Specially, there are many similar potential interview competitors to apply to the position at the same time. Otherwise, internet recruiting is not all positive. Such as some applicants skill place great value in face-to-face interactions in the hiring process. Such applicant's are likely to ignore jobs posted, impersonally on time.

I shall indicate these sample recruitment strategy to explain how to influence every applicant's choice to apply the job or not apply the job as below:

The first is online recruiting. This online recruitment strategy has a large percentage of employees are hired by human service agencies for every level jobs are seeking their first career job. The newspaper want ads are not an effective recruitment source for most of today's applicants. Placing vacancy announcements online is more effective and economical than using most traditional forms of advertising. However, online recruitment is designed to close this gap: Not reaching majority of applicants, especially young graduates.

The second is campus recruiting and job fairs. This campus recruiting strategy attracts both professional and paraprofessional applicants, who can be effectively recruited at job fairs sponsored by state workforce development agencies. However, college recruiting can be a very effective method for attracting applicants for professional jobs. The possible psychological advantages to applicants that includes any employers will send team of HR representatives to any colleges to provide an opportunity for job seekers to ask both job specific and hiring process/benefits questions; sending an ambassador to classrooms to quest lecture; schedule experienced employees or supervisors to ask on a hot topic in the human or service field at a local college or university. However, this campus recruiting strategy has a large percentage of employees hired, but need to improve overall applicant.

The third is university partner developing a variety of recruitment strategy. University partnership benefits include to collaborate with university deans and professors to help student interest in the field as well as to develop program partially covering college tuition and other expenses of college students who agree to work for the human service agency for specified periods of time. Its recruitment strategy aims to develop a variety of recruitment strategies with area universities, community colleges and schools of social work to encourage students to pursue careers in the human services. It's weakness lacks enough applicants with specialized social work degrees.

The fourth recruitment strategy is target recruitment. Employers may used a more diverse workforce that better reflects the client population who serve. For example, employers may need to recruit employees with specific language skills or with specialized degrees , e.g. criminal juice. It' weakness lacks of diversity in targeted jobs.

The fifth recruitment strategy is internships. Interns sometimes are paid stipend, but in most instances interns are fulfilling an academic requirement of the college or university. Although supervisors and/or cause work staff must spend time supervising and training interns, the potential payoff is having a known applicant who is familiar with agency operations. Its weakness is needed to improve overall applicant pool.

The sixth recruitment strategy is maintain a pre-screened applicant pool. It has a pool of pre-screened, interviewed applicants always available to be called for a second interview with the hiring supervisor. When, using this approach, it's important to minimize the amount of time between the initial interview and the second interview to prevent top quality applicants from being hired human resources will need to do continuous recruiting and screening , even when there are no current vacancies. It's weaknesses include that some human services organizations delay hiring until staff vacancies reach crisis proportions. They than initiate a recruitment process that is designed to bring new employees on board as soon as possible . The unfortunate result is hiring employees who meet the minimum requirements, but nothing more. It also has too many applicants get hired with only the minimum credentials.

The seventh recruitment strategy is realistic job previews. Realistic job previews are designed to prevent applicants from taking jobs that who have life knowledge of or are not suited to perform. It is a recruiting tool is designed to reduce early turnover by communicating both the desirable and the undesirable aspects of a jobs before applicants accept a job offer. It can be in the form of videos, oral presentations, job shadowing opportunities. It's weakness includes unwanted turnover among new workers who did not understand their job when who were hired.

The final recruitment strategy is improved hiring flexibilities in highly centralized systems. It means many public-sector human service agencies are regulated by merit systems that make it different to attract and maintain the interest of top-qualify applicants. Top applicants in today's economy are searching the interest for jobs that are available now. They aren't interested in taking a civil service exam and sitting on eligibility lists for months. In some systems requirements and lengthy inflexible scoring processes wash out well qualified applicants. It's weaknesses include hiring process takes too long, high qualify applicants are looking elsewhere for jobs.

- How to apply occupational psychological test method to test applicant's ability?

Occupational psychological interview method is the application of the science of psychology to test applicant individual work ability. For example, any interviews can apply occupational psychologists' test method to attempt to test applicant individual performance, motivation and wellbeing of the organization in the workplace. If any interviewers can attempt to apply occupational psychologist test method to test any applicant individual working abilities in interview. It brings this question: How can the interviewer develop, apply and evaluate a range of tools and interventions to test the applicant individual working abilities across many different areas of the workplace?

The occupational psychological test method can include these psychological skills to test every applicant individual ability in interview. Such as : Psychological assessment means selecting and assessing the applicant individual ability using interview enquiring method, e.g. in interview, enquiring applicant concerns on how to solve crisis deal issues when challenges cause in any workplace, assessments of what the applicant's main ability centers are. Situational judgement tests, e.g. how to solve challenges in different situations and personality questionnaires and cognitive ability tests. Profiling jobs are matching requirements to the applicant's future performance. Developing and choosing is valid, reliable, fair and suitable selectin procedures.

Thus, the psychological enquiring questions can concern on work motivation, performance, appraisal and management, leadership power influence and negotiation, employee engagement and commitment, citizenship and positive behaviors or counterproductive in workplace, psychology of group teams and teamwork different aspects, which have similar points , such as concern organizational behavior questions. It aims to test the applicant how to deal any immediate crisis in the organization if the interviewer decides to employ him/her.

The key focus of how to achieve one effective psychological test to the applicant in the interview. It focuses on key areas , such as the applicant personal goal attainment, interview performance, the applicant's mind on innovation and creativity aspects, and well being in the workplace how the applicant explains who will perform supposes who did the job in the workplace. In the interview, the interviewer needs the applicant to explain to let him/her to understand how the applicant's relation and motivation in the organization. The interviewer also needs to know how the applicant can solve any challenges in workplace in the situation test interview. Because conflict resolution is a challenging environment to work in. However, any downsides are offset by the rewards of being able to help protect both the organization and its employees from the psychological , physiological and economic costs of conflict. Because conflict will occur in possible in any workplaces. Thus, the interviewer ought to ask the question to let him/her to know the applicant will solve if who did this position.

Human factors is a discipline concerned with how the successful interview applicant (future employee) works effectively and safely. It considers a employee's environmental , organizational, job and individual characteristics. These factors will affect the organizational successful interview applicant (future employee) behavior and it is past of the interviewer's job to analyze these and to give recommendations for change to improve human performance to the organization if who selected to employ these applicants in every time interview. Thus it seems occupational psychological test method can give benefits to the interviewer to understand more to the applicants to judge whether who will be the most suitable applicant(s)to do any positions in whose organization more accurate decision in any interviews.

SEVEN

SELECTING AND EVALUATING ASSESSMENT METHODS

How selection assessment methods are applied to choose the best applicants ? Organizations compete in the war for talent. So, one effective selection assessment method can help any organizations to choose the best applicant(s). Using scientifically proven assessments to make selection decisions, even though such assessments have been shown to result in significant productivity increases, cost savings, decrease other critical organizational outcomes. I shall indicate common misconceptions about selection tests, such as: Screening applicants for conscientiousness will yield better performers , then screening applicants for intelligence, screening applicants for their values will yield better performers , then screening applicants for intelligence, integrity tests are not useful because job candidates misrepresent themselves on these types of tests, unstructured interviews with candidates provide better information than structured assessment processes and using selection tests creates legal problems for organizations rather than helps to solve them.

There are numerous different types of formal assessments that organizations can use to select employees. The first step in developing or selecting an assessment method for a given situation is to understand what the job requires employees to do and what knowledge, skills and abilities individuals must posses in order to perform the job effectively. This is typically accomplished by conducting a job analysis . For job oriented job analysis recruitment example, providing test by stating fact and answer questions, gathering and reviewing information to obtain evidence or develop background information on subjects, integrating diverse information to uncover relationships between individuals, events or evidences.

Other assessment methods focus on how measuring the best applicant who are required to perform job tasks effectively, such as various mental abilities, physical abilities or personality traits, depending on the job's requirements. If one were to assess whether candidates could solve decisive and communicate effectively. Alternatively, if one were selecting an administrative assistant, such as the ability to perform work conscientiously with speed and accuracy would be such more important for identifying capable candidates. Some worker-oriented or job analysis data are used as a basis for developing assessment method, that focus on a job candidate's underlying abilities to perform important work task.

In general, any organization interviews only divide either internal or external both selection. Internal selection refers to situations where organization is hiring or promoting from within, whereas, external selection refers to situations where an organization is hiring from the outside. When some assessment methods are used more commonly for external selection. (e.g. cognitive ability tests, personality tests, integrity tests). There are numerous examples of organizations that have used one or more of the following tools for internal selection, external selection or both. I shall explain what the differences for these interview test methods as follow:

What is cognitive ability tests. These assessment measure a variety of mental abilities, such as verbal and mathematical ability, reasoning ability and reading comprehension. Cognitive ability tests have been shown to be extremely useful predictors of job performance and thus are used frequently in making selection decisions for many different types of jobs (Hunter, J. 1986, Ree, M.J. & Teachout, M.S. 1984, Gottredson, L.S. 1982).

Cognitive ability tests typically consist of multiple choice items that are administered via a paper-and-pencil instructment or computer. Some cognitive ability tests contain test items that need various abilities, e.g. verbal ability, number ability etc. But then sum up the correct answers to all of the items to obtain a single total score. The total score then represents a measure of general mental ability. If a separate score is computed for each of the specific types of abilities, then the resulting scores represent measures of the specific mental abilities.

Job knowledge tests mean these assessments measure critical knowledge areas that are needed to perform a job effectively. Typically, the knowledge areas measured represent technical knowledge. Job knowledge tests are used in situations m where candidates must clearly possess a body of knowledge prior to job entry. Job knowledge tests are not appropriate to use in situations where candidates will be trained after selection on the on knowledge areas who need to have. Like cognitive ability tests, job knowledge tests typically consist of multiple-choice items administered via a paper-and-pencil instrument or a computer , although essay items are sometimes included in job knowledge tests (Hunter, J. 1986).

Personality tests that assess traits relevant to job performance have been shown to be effective predictors of subsequent job performance. The personality factors that are assessed most frequently in work situations include conscientiousness, extraversion, agreeableness, openness to experience and emotional stability (Barrick, M.R. & Mount, M.K. 1991, Costa, P.T. Jr., & Mccae, r. R. 1982).

Research has shown that conscientiousness is the most useful predictor of performance across many different jobs. Although some of the other personal factors have been shown to be useful predictors of performance in specific types of jobs (Hough, L.M. 1992). It can consist of several multiple choice or true/false items measuring each personality factor. Like cognitive ability and knowledge tests, which are also administered in a paper-and-pencil or computer format.

Biographical data (biodata) inventories, which ask job candidates questions covering their background, personal characteristics or interests have been shown to be effective predictors of job performance (Stokes, G.S. & Owens, W.A. 1994, Shoenfeldt, L.F. 1999). Another form of a biodata inventory is an instrument called an " accomplishment stored". With this types of assessment, candidates prepare a written account of their most meritorious accomplishments in key skill and ability areas that are required for a job , e.g. planning and organizing, customer service, conflict resolution (Hough, L.M. 1984).

Integrity tests measure attitudes and experiences that are related to an individual honesty, trustworthiness and dependability (Sackett, P.R. & Wanek, J.E. 1996). It is typically multiple-choice in format and administered via a paper-and-pencil instrument or a computer.

Physical fitness tests are used in some selection situations. These tests require candidates to perform general physical activities to assess one's overall fitness, strength or other physical capabilities necessary to perform the job.

Situational judgement tests provide job candidates with situations that who would encounter on the job and viable options for handling the presented situations (Mecichmann, D., Schmitt, N. & Harvey, V.S. 2001). depending on how the test is designed , candidates are asked to select the most effective or most and least effective ways of handling the situation from the response options provided. Situational judgement tests are more complicated to develop than many of the other types of assessments. It is because more difficulty in developing scenarios with several likely response options that are all viable, but in fact, some are reliably rated as being more effective than others. Situational judgement tests are typically administered in written or paper-and-pencil test booklet or on a computer.

Assessment centers are a type of work sample test that is typically focused on assessing higher-level managerial and supervisory competencies (Thornton, G.C III 1992). Assessment centers usually last at least a day and up to several days. They typically include role-play exercises in -basket exercises, analytical exercises and group discussion exercises. Trained assessors observe the performance of candidates during the assessment process and evaluate them on standardized rating. Some assessment centers also include other types of assessment methods, such as cognitive ability, job knowledge and personality tests. It should be noted selection purposes that assessment centers aren't only used for comprehensive development feedback to participants.

Physical ability tests are used regularly to select workers for physically demanding jobs, such as police officers and firefighters. These test are similar to work sample tests in that who typically require candidates to perform a series of actual job tasks to determine whether or not who can perform the physical requirements of a jobs. Physical ability tests are often scored in a pass/fail basis. To pass, the complete set of take that comprise the test must be properly completed within a specified timeframe.

● How to criteria for selecting and evaluating assessment methods in interview?

Properly identifying and implementing formed assessment methods to select employees is one of the more complex areas for HR department to learn about and understand. This is because understanding selection testing requires knowledge of statistics, measurement issues and legal issues relevant to testing.

I recommend any interviewers need to understand important criteria to decide to choose which kind of interview test is the suitable to test applicant individual abilities in every interview such as below:

The first criteria includes validity. Validity means the extent to which the assessment method is useful for predicting subsequent job performance. Adverse impact means the extent to which protected group members , e.g. minorities, females and individuals over 40 score lower on the assessment than majority group members.

The second criteria includes cost. Cost is both to develop and to administer the assessment. Applicant reactions means the extent to which applicants react positively versus negatively to the assessment method. For example, cognitive ability test. on the positive side, this type of assessment is high on validity and low on costs. However, it is also high on adverse impact, moderately favorable. Thus, when cognitive tests are inexpensive and very useful for predicting subsequent job performance, score significantly lower on them than whites. There is no simple, formulaic approach for selecting " one best" assessment method, because all of them have advantages and disadvantages.

However, the most important consideration in evaluating on assessment method is its validity. Validity refers to whether or not the assessment method provides useful information about how effectively an employee will actually perform once who is hired for a job. Validity is the most important factor in considerate whether or not to use an assessment method because identify who will doesn't accurately identify who will perform effectively on a job has no value to the organization.

There are two major forms of validity: criterion-related validity and content validity is a simple example will illustrate how criterion-related validity can be established. Assume that a sales job requires employees to have a high level of customer service orientation and an organization decides to implement a selection test that assesses prospective applicants on their customer service skills. In order to show that the client skills assessment is a valid predictor of performance , it must be shown that individuals who score higher on the assessment perform better. On the job and individuals who score lower on the assessment perform less well on the job. Thus, validity in this case would be defined as a meaningful relationship between how well people performed on the assessment and how well who subsequently performed on the job. Content validity approach to validation involves demonstrating that an assessment provides a direct measure of how well candidates will actually perform to job. This type of validation requires analyzing the job to identify the tasks that are performed.

What are the differences between criterion related versus content validation. Criterion-related validity can be used to evaluate the validity of any assessment where individuals receive scores that reflect how well who perform on the test and these scores are subsequently shown to relate to how well who perform on the job. Content validation can only be used to validate assessments that provide a direct measure of how well candidates perform job tasks or the content of the jobs, such as work sample tests. Otherwise, criterion-related validity evidence or validity . Thus, it is more desirable to obtain if it is possible to conduct a successful unbiased performance measures must be available. Unfortunately, performance appraisal ratings, which are the most commonly used performance measures can be inaccurate and often fail.

Adverse impact is examined by comparing the proportion of majority group who are selected from a job to the protected group members who are selected. When organizations are and should be interested in selecting the higher quality work force possible, many are also concerned about selecting a diverse workforce ought not using measures that will systematically produce adverse impact against protected groups.

In conclusion, either if an assessment method is shown to produce adverse impact and the organization wished to continue the last of that assessment, there are legal requirements to ensure that the method must have demonstrated validity or if an organization uses an assessment that produces adverse impact that produces adverse impact without the validity evidence. The organization will encounter challenges against which it won't be able to prevail. When evidence of validity can be used to justify and defend the use of measures that produce an adverse impact many organizations nonetheless attempt to apply the adverse impact produced be their assessment methods to extent possible in order to minimize potential interview wrong recruitment decisions and lack of diversity concerns issues to recruit any the most suitable applicants to do any positions in any organizations.

Reference

Barrick, M. R. & Mount , M.K. (1991). The big five personality dimensions and job performance: A meta-analysis, personnel psychology, 91, 1-26.

Costa, P.T. & Jr., & McCrae, R.R. (1992). Four ways five factors are basic. Personality and individual differences, 13, 653-665.

Gottredson, L.S. (Ed). (1982). The g factor in employment, Journal of vacational behavior, 29(3).

Hough, L.. (1992) The big five personality variables construct confusion: Description versus prediction human performance, 5, 135-155.

Hough, L.M. (1984). Development and evaluation of the " accomplishment record" methods of selecting and promoting professonals. Journal of applied psychology, 69, 135-146.

Hunter, J. (1986). Cognitive ability, cognitive aptitudes, job knowledge and job performance, Journal of vacational behavior, 29, 340-362.

Meichmann, D., Schmitt, N., & Harvey, V.S. (20010. Incremental validity of situatinal judgement tests , Journal of applied psychology, 86, 410-417.

Ree, M.J. Earles, J.A., & Teachout, M.S. (1994), Predicting job performance: Hot much more than g. Journal of applied psychology, 79, 518-524.

Robserton, I. T., & Smith, M. (2001). Personnel Selection. Journal Of Occupational And Organizational Psychological Psychology, 74(4), 441-472.

Sackett, P.R. & Wanek, J.E. (1996). New developments in the use of measures of honesty, integrity, conscientiousness, dependability, trustworthiness and reliability for personnel selection, personnel psychology, 49, 787-829.

Schuler, Randalls, S: Personnel and human resources management. Third edition, 1987.

Shoenfeldt, L.F. (1999). From dustbowl empiricism to rational constructs in biodata. Human resource management review, 9, 147-167.

Steven, Kay Cynthia (1997). Effects of pre-interview beliefs on applicant's reactions to campus interviews. Academy of management journal, 40(4), 947-966.

Stokes, G.S. Mumford, M.D. & owen, W.A. (Eds.) (1994). Biodata handbook paloacto, CA: CPP Books.

Thornton, G.C. III (1992). Assessment centers in human resources management Addison-Wesley,

Whetton, D.A. & Cameron, K.S. (2002). Developing Management , Skill 5th edition, reading, MA: Addison Wesley Longman.

9 798887 728209

Printed by Libri Plureos GmbH in Hamburg, Germany